Priscilla Spoerer

PLEASE, LORD, UNTIE MY TONGUE...

...when there is illness, death, divorce, imprisonment

Kenneth A. Erickson

Publishing House
St. Louis

Copyright © 1983 Concordia Publishing House
3558 S. Jefferson Avenue, St. Louis, MO 63118

Printed in the United States of America

Library of Congress Cataloging in Publication Data

Erickson, Kenneth A.
    Please, Lord, untie my tongue—when there is illness, death, divorce, imprisonment.

    1. Visitations (Church work) I. Title. BV4320.E74 1983
253.5   82-14473
ISBN 0-570-03881-2 (pbk.)

---

1 2 3 4 5 6 7 8 9 10   WP   92 91 90 89 88 87 86 85 84 83

To all who seek to accept Jesus' invitation to visit the lonely and the hurting but who feel inexperienced and unqualified.

Contents

Preface 6
Acknowledgments 7
Introduction 9
1 When There Is Illness 11
2 When There Is Death 21
3 When There Is Divorce 33
4 When There Is Imprisonment 43
5 The Challenge 55

Preface

"I don't know what to say" is not an idle or weak rationalization. Many adults lack both experience and knowledge of words and actions that are appropriate when seeking to be part of the healing process for an acquaintance in distress.

Because we feel that we lack that experience and wisdom, we often find excuses to procrastinate such ministries. One common rationalization is simply, "I don't know what to say!" But our Lord exhorts us to action with His promise, "My grace is all you need, for My power is strongest when you are weak" (2 Corinthians 12:9 TEV).

The helpful ideas in this book will serve as a learning aid for those who wish to improve their visitation skills. I have compiled these suggestions from persons who have struggled with problems of illness, bereavement, divorce, or imprisonment. Their comments and advice will help us to understand and comfort our brothers and sisters in their distress.

Acknowledgments

Grateful acknowledgment is offered to many friends for their valuable input and counsel: William Adix, Linda Anderson, Larry Baker, Signe Bustad, John Craig, Donald Egge, Rolf Erickson, Robert Grover, Joanne Gulsvig, Doris Helikson, Jon Hellstedt, Michael Johnson, Virginia Klassen, Steve Lauch, Janette Mowery, June Regan, Marva Sedore, Fenton Sharpe, Bernice Skinner, Joyce Thelin, Roy Vernstrom, Sandy Young, and Stuart Young.

Special appreciation goes to my wife, Lois, whose continual encouragement and constructive reviews were vital to this publication. Jan Stark as manuscript typist was both capable and supportive.

Introduction

This book started with Sherm. We served together on the church council, where I admired his straightforward approach to issues.

Later Sherm became ill. The diagnosis was cancer. I wanted to visit him, but I really didn't know what to say. Yet Sherm's candor in relationships with his friends encouraged me to approach him the same way.

I drove to his home for my first visit. Maybe Sherm would be at the doctor's office. But he was home, and I think he discerned my difficulty. "Sherm," I said, "I need your help. I don't know what to say when I come to visit a friend who is sick. How about becoming my teacher in this area?"

Thus began a deeper, genuine relationship that influenced my life. Our talks were memorable because, like Sherm, they were without pretense. He proved to be an able teacher.

But I do have one regret. The experience of praying with a sick friend also was a new venture to me. Sherm knew I was praying *for* him. Yet, I determined to pray *with* him at my next visit. When I returned from several days out of town, however, it was too late. I had deferred too long, and Sherm was gone.

In conversing with friends later, I learned that many of them hesitate to visit the sick, the bereaved, the recently divorced, and the imprisoned because of feeling inadequate—they "don't know what to say." Sherm's instruction fostered my identification of ideas and actions, both helpful and unhelpful, related to visitation skills. I interviewed knowledgeable individuals, analyzed questionnaire results, arranged group discussions, and asked those experienced in these areas to evaluate the guidelines developed. Some group discussions were held in adult retreat centers—others were inside a county jail or in a state penitentiary. The primary sources for this book may be described as hurting persons, all of whom experience loneliness—the ill, the bereaved, the recently divorced, and the imprisoned.

You will hear their voices throughout this book.

1
When There Is Illness

As a preteenager, I was hospitalized with pneumonia. Al and Myrtle, a young married couple from church, were my only nonfamily visitors. I was impressed, almost embarrassed, with the fact they had driven a long distance to visit a youngster. They brought a gift I still remember—*Young Fu of the Upper Yangtze*, a book with beautiful gold lettering. Their remembrance of time and book said more to me than most lessons. Al and Myrtle's love and concern are a sermon I have never forgotten.

Many intend to visit the sick but are hesitant because they don't know what to say. Their good intentions go unfulfilled. One set of standards cannot be formulated to help every visitation. Each sick person is unique—each illness differs in its effect. General guidelines, though, can inspire sincere persons to visit the ill. Conscientious individuals will be able to adapt the following principles to the personal needs and distress level of each patient.

Visitation Length and Timing

The timing of visits to patients can help or hinder their recovery. Check in advance with the family to determine if visits are welcome and what the recommended length is. It is generally best to wait at least two days after major surgery. Gauge the length of a visit and the depth of the conversation by the severity of the illness and apparent energy level of the patient.

Pressures felt by the ill to "entertain" guests may be exhausting. Prolonged visits can lower the patient's natural resistance to disease and delay recovery. The sick are dependent on each visitor's good judgment regarding the length of call. One former patient reported, "I enjoyed my visitors and tended to encourage their stay for a longer time than was helpful. I wasn't in a position to know what was right for me, and later I suffered from exhaustion."

Sensitivity to the strength of the patient *at the moment* of the visit is critical. Another friend said, "During recovery from a surgery, I didn't tire so easily. During a different illness, an hour's visit brought on another attack and a serious setback."

One patient remarked that a caller told him, "I saw the NO VISITORS sign on your door, but I didn't think it meant me." For the patient's welfare, respect the NO VISITORS sign. Regardless of notices on the patient's door, it is a sensible practice always to inquire at the nurses' station. Occasionally, the NO VISITORS warning is there to control the flow, rather than to stem it completely.

Plan your visits when the least number of guests might be expected. Avoid large group gatherings. A number of friends calling at the same time may unwittingly enjoy an informal get-together that tires the patient. Should several friends be present on your arrival, wait outside or make a short stay. The value of a "look-in" visit should not be underrated—it need not be impersonal, but can communicate "I'm concerned, but I also recognize your need for time by yourself."

Comfort of the Patient

Knock before entering the hospital room. Respect the fact that your friend needs some privacy. Also identify yourself immediately on entering the room. This is helpful should the patient be sleepy or somewhat sedated.

Be very gentle. While it can be healing to touch the patient's hand, forgo a handshake that is at all forceful. Avoid bumping or even touching the bed or other items of equipment around the patient. Even a slight jar may be disconcerting, painful, or in some way harmful.

Don't hesitate to introduce the theme of some reading you've found interesting or helpful. Ask about specific reading material the patient may prefer, but resist the temptation to prescribe certain books for reading.

The visitor faces a perplexing problem, when entering a room, if the patient seems to be sleeping. It is hard to know whether the patient is asleep, is drowsing and would welcome a reason to be awake, or is tired and trying to avoid company. Unless you feel comfortable just sitting quietly in the room, retreat is usually the best policy.

Hospital stays today tend to be minimal in length. Patients are discharged earlier than in previous years. Just because an acquaintance has returned home, don't expect him or her to be upbeat, chipper, and energetic. Without implying that the patient is helpless, offer some concrete assistance, such as taking the person to the doctor, fixing a meal, doing the dishes, mowing the lawn, or cleaning part of the house. As one former patient said, "We don't like to be forgotten during posthospital convalescence. Home visits, written notes, or phone calls are all supportive and beneficial."

Communicating Verbally with Patients

Regard a person's illness as his or her own "property" that is not subject to appropriate handling by everybody. Patients may choose to share their property with you, but should never be questioned in such a way that they have no choice.

Resist the natural tendency to overcommunicate—to fill all the silent moments. Though it may seem difficult, you need say very little in most situations. Your presence is more meaningful than your words—and less demanding on the patient. Hushed listening cherishes your friend. If not sure what to say, touch the patient's hand and assert, "I know this is not easy for you, but I am with you—I care about you and will remember you in my prayers."

A former patient reported, "During two extended illnesses, I valued the friend who dropped in casually, asked directly how I was faring, and then talked of friends we share as well as interesting community events. However, it was not helpful if guests detailed recent surgeries or other illnesses, assuming that would take my mind off my own situation." Well-meaning comments, however, such as "God has a reason for this" or "God allowed this for a purpose" sound judgmental to the ailing person. They evidence an immodest lack of sensitivity to God's unique involvement in each patient's life.

Encourage the patient to look to the future with invitations such as, "When you're out of the hospital and really feel up to it, perhaps we can plan a drive up the McKenzie River Highway." It would be inappropriate, though, to make such offers to a person who is obviously facing death and knows it.

A friend who had been seriously ill shared the following helpful experience. "In the middle of the night a nurse took time to listen for a while as I voiced my concerns and worries. She did nothing more than sit on the bed, hold my hand, listen attentively, and be reassuring. This was the turning point of my illness."

Nonverbal Communication with the Patient

Send attractive cards with a pleasant, inspirational message. Add some personal thoughts to make your note more meaningful. A homemade greeting with a light touch of humor often is appreciated. Including a Scripture verse can make your communication especially personal. Some so-called "religious inspiration" cards can be heavy-handed.

When entering the patient's room, be prepared for the fact that your friend could appear to be worsening. Should that be the situation, avoid expressions of surprise that could give the signal that you believe something is seriously wrong. Avoid any conversation with another guest in hushed tones in one corner of the patient's room or in the hall outside the door.

Bringing a gift to one who is ill evidences your caring. One former patient disclosed, "To me a little gift always represented God's love in action; a concrete expression of affection that befriends me 24 hours a day (e.g., a small teddy bear that clings to my bed, larger stand-up cards, plants, flowers, etc.)." Paul Tournier in his book, *The Meaning of Gifts*, writes that the significance of a gift is found in the nonverbal love it expresses.

Some churches make several smaller bouquets from the altar flowers and take them to the ill and shut-ins with the Sunday bulletin. It is prudent, though, to avoid bringing plants or flowers with a strong, overpowering fragrance. Also, inquire in advance about possible allergy problems.

Another former patient reported, "One friend brought his cassette tape player with earphones—also tapes of relaxing music, good humor, and some inspirational messages. These helped me use my time when I was too exhausted or concerned to do any reading."

Knowing the patient as you do, thoughtfully adapt any gift to your friend's interests. This could include special foods, if approved by the doctor. A simple, useful gift, can be notepaper, stamped envelopes, and a pen.

"When my pastor visited me," said one former patient, "he reached over and took hold of my hand. There is something special about the human touch, even for five or ten seconds, that I found both nourishing and comforting."

Prayer and the Patient

Before entering a patient's room, pray that you and your visit may be used by God for the good of the one who is ill.

One pastor advised that, "Prayer with patients can be a ticklish thing. For some it suggests a critical status and thus may be more frightening than supportive. A sensitive visitor, though, can suggest prayer when the patient is an acquaintance. Even pastors, who are expected to quote Scripture and pray, need to be perceptive in this area."

Whatever the prayer needs are, they should be fulfilled in a personal and nurturing manner. One former patient found it unhelpful when a visitor "launched into loud, emotional prayer that was much too long and tiresome to be renewing."

A brief, appropriate prayer with the patient may simply be for his or her continual progress and return to health. One patient stated, "How supportive it is to hear that many friends are remembering me in their prayers! It's also very reinforcing when the visitor has a short prayer with me before leaving."

Prayer was important to another friend who shared this experience. "I was feeling emotionally low when I received a late evening phone call from a friend who is a busy senator in Washington, D.C. He reported he had been checking on me with the hospital almost daily and had conducted prayer sessions for me with his staff. Then he closed his phone call with a prayer I'll never forget!"

Ministering to the Severely Ill

In a real sense, everyone alive today is "terminal." Treat a patient with a life-threatening illness not as one you have consigned to die but as the living person he or she continues to be.

"Most important to me," said one patient, "is the need to have my family and friends deal honestly and openly with me about my severe illness." Many agree that the cruelest way to treat a patient known to be terminal is to offer false hopes. Family members who keep a serious diagnosis from an ailing person may do so for self-serving reasons, being fearful of facing the inevitability of a loved one's death. But the ailing usually resent being kept ignorant in this critical area. Aware of the facts, they often wish to write special letters, arrange to see dear friends, and make a number of decisions very important to them.

Is it possible to minister to a patient who is completely lethargic? A woman had suffered a severe stroke and *appeared* not to know anybody or to hear anything. She lay impassively for weeks. The family did not know whether she was aware of their visits and communication. Then a friend brought a tape of Christian hymns that had been very familiar during her childhood. In this situation it proved to be the first external stimulus to which she responded.

Another friend shared the following experience in relation to her husband's final illness. "The nurses used to say that even during my brief visits with him in the intensive care unit it would be helpful to talk and tell him anything to encourage mental stimulation. But after so many hours and days by his bedside, I had depleted the loving topics I wanted to share. Now I wish I had thought of this idea earlier when it may have been helpful. I wish I had taken the previous year's Christmas letters we had saved to answer—the family picture albums—the scrapbooks of our trips—

his retirement scrapbook—a little at a time to share with him and to promote his mental stimulation."

Visitors from the church family, the patient's own community of faith, are always a special source of nourishment and support. Be prepared to sit quietly and listen if your friend wishes to share any concerns or fears. Just be at ease with the patient, letting the conversation flow and ebb. Even if you sit in silence for a while, your presence still speaks of your continuing support and God's enfolding love.

2
When There Is Death

We learned of our foster son's death on Friday. A fellow church member about our son's age heard the news through the prayer fellowship. Early Saturday morning, our door bell rang. Our friend stood on the porch holding a bouquet of pink plum blossoms and yellow daffodils.

"I'm sorry about your son," he said as he handed me the flowers. "I brought my wheelbarrow and shovel to help move that load of chicken fertilizer from the driveway to your garden." I don't recall much he said in words that morning, but I'll never forget what he said in actions. His kindness embodied God's loving care in our time of need.

How often we neglect the distress of the bereaved because we "don't know what to say." In doing so, we deprive them of our supportive presence and compassion. Our society seems void of reminders that friends may still be working through grief. Funeral services are abbreviated. Mourning clothes are no longer the custom. The recognition of a definite time for grieving has been annulled.

The grief response follows a series of typical steps but has no predetermined schedule. Shock, numbness, denial, anger, and a questioning of God's love are all normal. These come in unpredictable waves but typically must be worked through over a period of time for the healing procedure to be successful.

Communication: Verbal

A friend who has lost a loved one needs to talk. This is essential to working through grief. We are simply to listen in love and affirm our continuous caring. We needn't be fearful whether we say the 'right' things. Our presence at their time of distress speaks of our sincere concern.

Be natural in talking with family members. Don't avoid using the words "dead" or "death." Normally it is our personal queasiness that keeps us from direct communication. The same holds with regard to the dead person's name. We hesitate saying the name, lest we bring up an emotional subject. As one widow said, though, "Mention my husband's name with a happy incident or memory. Bring up something really funny or dear, and I'll find myself laughing."

In an article, "Helping Her Cry," Ronald Combs writes of a person who detailed how much she missed her neighbor's husband and the way they used to stand by the old fence, tell jokes, and laugh. After this exchange, the widow said, "Thanks for making my day so much brighter. I don't understand why—but people never talk to me about Max. They think it will make me feel sad. But what wonderful memories it brings back, and it makes the sorrow of his absence a little less." Combs adds that it is helpful for survivors to realize that their loved ones were important to others.

A man in our congregation was killed in an accident. The neighbor next door said to the surviving wife, "I told my son that he would never meet a gentler man than your husband!" Later the wife shared her reaction to that neighbor's comment. "It's important to hear about the good things others saw in your loved one's life."

"Bring up specific incidents involving the one who has died," said another person. "When my pilot brother-in-law died, flight officers and stewardesses phoned or wrote with specific instances of how he had been of help with various problems. These stories were treasured by his wife as she shared them with family members. Such positive communication is extremely comforting."

Refrain from bestowing unrequested advice on survivors (e.g., get rid of personal effects, sell the house, take a trip, sell some furniture when you're ready and I'll buy it, etc.).

If you have had an identical experience, it may be acceptable to comment to the bereaved, "I think I know where you are, and I've come through it."

Otherwise, be very honest in your communication and say, "I haven't had the same experience, so I really can't know how you feel, but I do care about you. That's why I am here."

Declaring to the survivor, "It was God's will, no doubt," often hurts, if not embitters the person in distress. In contrast, one friend comforted the bereaved with, "When our spiritual eyes are open, we undoubtedly would see Jesus standing at your elbow weeping with you over the loss of your loved one."

Communication: Written

Often we are overly concerned about "saying the right thing" in sympathy letters. Our concern about doing the wrong thing often results in procrastination or complete inaction. It is better to write letters promptly while your feelings are genuine. Sincerity is more important than letter length.

Communicating meaningful memories in a letter shares experiences the bereaved will cherish for years. One acquaintance disclosed, "I lost my mother when I was 24. The letters from older people described special memories of my mother I had not known. What treasures they are! They had known my mother as a child, though I had no previous contact with them." Another friend recounted this experience. "It was too far to go to his funeral, so I wrote a letter to his wife recounting everything that was meaningful in our association and why he had meant so much to me. Later she responded declaring, 'Your letter was so comforting because it pinpointed many wonderful, specific relationships.'"

Identify yourself in any communication with the survivor. One friend said, "I received many cards and notes... several from people I did not know... though they knew my husband. If you are not known to the spouse, it is helpful to indicate how and where you knew the person."

A friend of mine was seriously ill. His wife received an original and nourishing type of communication in the form of 3 x 5 cards on which were written the following Bible verses: 1 Corinthians 13:12-13; 2 Corinthians 4:16-17 and 5:2, 5, 8; Romans 8:22-23; and 1 Peter 5:7. She added, "I carried these in my purse and referred to them often. I read them to my husband during the hospitalization. After his death, they also were so helpful to me."

Silent Communication: Nonverbal actions

A grieving friend states, "Reality for me had gone out; unreality had come in. I desperately needed other persons to be with me in these new, strange, fearful circumstances." What I might say to the bereaved is less important than the personal sharing of my time. Survivors may scarcely notice what others say, but they do appreciate their friend's willingness to be present.

A story illustrating the importance of being with others tells of a five-year-old girl whose dearest friend had died. On her return from visiting her friend's mother, someone asked her what she had said. "I didn't say anything," she replied. "I just sat on her lap and cried with her!"

While we may feel uneasy about what to say when we see the bereaved, the important fact is that we are there and we care. It is the gift of personal time evidenced by our presence that is most needed. We also are supportive when we put our arms around the person or hold their hand.

In a letter to "Dear Abby," a widow emphasized that those who did come to visit really ministered to her in her sorrow. On the other hand she interpreted the actions of friends who made no contact as an "I don't care" feeling. Her advice to those unsure of what to say is that a simple "I'm sorry" is sufficient. "Believe me," she continued, "your face and eyes express the feelings you can't put into words." To her the most meaningful communication came in the form of hugs, pats on the shoulder, and squeezes on the hand together with the statement, "I just don't know what to say." "They didn't realize it," she concluded, "but they already had said it all."

An acquaintance who had lost a spouse said, "I was having lunch with a friend who was unaware of the recent death in our family. On learning of it, she reached across the table, took my hand, and held it for 5 to 10 minutes. Normally, a very busy person, her actions emphasized that she would sit in silence with me for eternity, were that helpful. It was like we were taking 'time out of time.'"

Normally it is a polite but empty offer to declare, "If I can do anything, let me know." This is best illustrated by Dorothy Hsu's poem, "Don't Say."

> Don't say,
> "If you need anything, call."
> I need all sorts of things,
> But I won't call.
> I'm not built that way.
> You call me.
> Tell me:
> "I'll pick up the girls today."
> Tell me:
> "Bob will be over to mow the lawn."
> Tell me:
> "I'll help you clean today."
> But don't say,
> "If you need anything, call."

There are other helpful activities that correspond with Dorothy Hsu's thinking. "One of the things I really appreciated was someone asking if they could make some phone calls for me. I took care of the relatives and close friends, but there are others someone else can take care of." Or if older persons have no car, offer to drive to the various offices he or she must contact. The elderly especially need lots of support.

"On the day before my husband's funeral," a friend related, "a Mennonite lady who knew my husband in the hospital voluntarily came to our house to help with such things as ironing the clothes we were to wear, polishing the children's shoes, and so forth. I felt cushioned by her concern." Another person wrote: "Three elderly friends came over the day before the memorial service and cleaned my house. They also served the potluck dinner after the service."

Miscellaneous offers of supportive ministry include: "I'll take your laundry home with me." "Please phone me anytime you feel like talking." "I'll go to the cemetery office with you." "I'll stay in your house during the funeral."

Dealing with Feelings

We may feel ill at ease with shocked and worried friends who are working through grief. Yet we minister supportively when we allow them to express their true feelings to us and when we give them permission to cry. Conversely, we are unhelpful if we urge the grieving person to mask or repress true feelings—to "be strong." Those who deny or bottle up their emotions have greater difficulty working through grief than those who openly admit and air their feelings.

The parental admonition, "Boys don't cry," is inconsistent with Scriptural wisdom, which counsels us: "Weep with those who weep." There is real enfolding in the willingness of a friend to weep with a sorrowing person. It is vital that those who have lost loved ones be gently and lovingly liberated to cry, particularly if they are hiding behind a mask to maintain an undaunted front.

Prayer and Grace

Before contacting the bereaved, ask God for some comprehension of your friend's sorrow, so that you bring comfort in adversity.

Let those who mourn know that you are upholding them in prayer. Also, nourish those who grieve by praying with them. This is a substantial source of comfort and helps them with their burden.

If we mortals hear of others we scarcely know tell of their sorrows and we feel like enfolding them to cushion their grieving, how much more does God through Christ love and support those who mourn! Furthermore, we can affirm to survivors that in death God already has given the perfect healing to wasted bodies, a basis for mingling praise and joy with heartache.

No human relationship is perfect. Did any of us ever do everything we wished to for a loved one—or never do anything thoughtless or hurtful? In regretting the past a griever may carry some unresolved guilt that could be harmful unless alleviated. Freedom from regret becomes a reality when we help those who sorrow base their faith in our caring heavenly Father, who through Jesus Christ continually evidences complete love, complete forgiveness, and complete acceptance of us just as we are.

Postfuneral Loneliness

"I will be forever grateful to the women of our

congregation for the food at the church after the funeral," a member of our church family emphasized. "It gave those attending an opportunity to express their care and concern in a personal way and the family an opportunity to acknowledge and respond. It provided just the right closing for the service. But it would help if those bringing food either used disposable containers or dishes marked with their name."

Another person said, "We were overwhelmed with food the first two or three days. We couldn't enjoy it all then. Later nobody seemed to remember that you might not feel like fixing anything. *Then* a dish of food would be far more welcome." In a similar vein another individual said: "One of the strongest needs for me is not to have everyone disappear on me when I need them most, after all the relatives have gone."

Sunday usually is the loneliest day of all. It's a family day and a difficult one on which to be alone. One grieving person elaborated, "After my father passed away, my mother and I were alone at the house the following Sunday. We waited all afternoon for someone to come. It was a letdown; nothing happened. Later a number of friends reported, 'We knew you would have a lot of company in the afternoon, so we didn't come.'"

Another person who lost her husband shared the struggle she had returning to her family church. "Perhaps the most difficult adjustment I had was to continue attendance at my own church services. The thought of going into the building all alone, being alone when greeted—feeling unable to sit in the regular place—and wondering where to go for dinner afterwards seemed more than I could face. I still felt the need for church, so I went out of town to be with relatives—or took unchurched people and visited another church—or went to downtown churches taking elderly people who normally listened to sermons on their home radio. Then two couples invited me to our church retreat. Attending lectures, eating together, hiking, visiting, etc. took me 'over the hump.' I've been able to attend my church ever since."

Holidays, birthdays, and Christmas are times when one particularly misses a partner. It is helpful if others demonstrate their care by a visit, a call, or an invitation. Don't let survivors be alone on the anniversary of the death. At such times memories sweep over the survivors. Phone them. Take them out to dinner. Talk with them about the person who died (unless they indicate they don't wish to).

There is potential healing for survivors in doing things for others—even in their time of personal need. Invite grieving persons to join you in some assistance to others. It may offer an opportunity to step away from the natural reaction of self-pity. On the other hand, realize that the survivor may be exhausted—mentally, physically, and emotionally. While diplomatically informing them of the needs of others, allow them to decide when they feel able to "give" again.

Special community groups can be nourishing and reinforcing to those distressed by the death of a loved one. Survivors may be unaware of the specific help available from groups such as Widow-Widower, Compassionate Friends, and Theos (an acronym for "They Help Each Other Spiritually). In many communities other local groups have similar goals.

The helping servant who enfolds the hurting friend in love represents more than himself or herself to the survivor. As one friend emphasized, "I will ever be grateful for the many kindnesses shown to me and my family after my husband's death. They not only made a difficult time bearable—they also made the presence of God a reality."

3

When There Is Divorce

"After my divorce," the young woman told me, "some people treated me as if I had a contagious disease. It tore me apart. I already had feelings of guilt, shame, and failure. What I desperately needed from others was some evidence of the Good News in action—love, acceptance, and forgiveness. Then one friend said, 'To me you have not changed as a person. I still care about you very much.' I thanked God for that expression of caring. It was His love incarnate in a follower of Christ."

Divorce needs to be recognized as more than the death of a human bond. Usually it is the climax of a stress-filled, deteriorating relationship.

Understanding the Divorced Person's Experience

"I existed in a conversational vacuum for years because many did not talk with me about my divorce," one person commented. "Friends treated a significant event in my life like a white elephant sitting in the middle of the room—yet in their conversation everyone ignored the subject. Disregarding a major event is worse than saying the wrong thing about it."

Another friend explained, "So much of our tradition is based on couples and families. The divorced person has lost not just a spouse but family gatherings and much of the children's time, often on special holidays."

Each spouse is an uncommon individual and each divorce a unique event. Friends need to be sensitive, therefore, to the distinctive feelings of each separated individual. Divorce accentuates the heartache and pain if a spouse feels deserted. Divorce may bring a sense of relief if a person felt ill-treated or oppressed during marriage. But every divorced person experiences loneliness and needs the ministering love of supportive friends in the church family.

Trying to comfort a divorced person with "I know *just* how you feel" is not helpful. As one person declared, "Nobody knows *just* how anyone else feels. And even if they did, the divorce experience can be so painful that I would resent them saying so. The psychological pain and guilt of divorce tend to make you crawl off into some dark thicket of your mind like a wounded deer. Granted you need some solitude to listen to your emotions and thoughts, but the goal in befriending the divorced should be to help them heal and emerge—not to leave them to stiffen and die inside by closeting themselves in the thicket the rest of their days. After the companionship of a marriage, loneliness is the toughest adjustment to face." Similar feelings are expressed in the poem, "Winter":

> The icicle's tears drip constantly,
> You cry and cry and never seem to cry-out
>   the spring that begets the river
>   of sorrow.
> The trees, bent under their habit of
>   white,
> Can only stand and stare in silent
>   sympathy
> around me.

Some assert that the loss in divorce is worse than the loss in death. After death, one recalls good things about a person. After a loss through divorce, one tends to remember unhappy, hostile experiences. Divorce is a death that is never complete; it tends to recur with each family contact, after which the relationship dies all over again.

Feelings of guilt, shame, and failure continue after a marriage breakup. One friend explained, "I felt rejected, degraded, used—and yes, I felt I had failed my spouse." Church family members who have not walked in the shoes of a divorced person need to avoid feelings of superiority or judgment. Such reactions contradict the needed Christian love, support, and acceptance.

Our Reaction—Judging or Accepting?

"Some church members treat me as if I had leprosy," alleged one person. "Even if that is not intended, I may misread and interpret their actions as rejection—especially if they fail to talk with me. Possibly they bypass me because they don't know what to say.

"But any rejection from friends only reopens the same old wound of being spurned by my spouse. Try, therefore, to welcome the divorced person with no less and with no more enthusiasm and sincerity than before."

Church members need to enfold rather than judge those who have been cut off from marital companionship. Even if at fault, the separated spouse is a bruised individual who hungers for a friend's total acceptance. Whether or not our personal standards reject divorce, we can accept hurting individuals with love, grace, and forgiveness. Christ gave us His model for enfolding the distressed. First He expressed His care and acceptance for the woman taken in adultery. Then He said, "Go and sin no more."

"One of the worst things that people do to one that is hurting," contended a friend, "is to road block them by saying things like 'You shouldn't feel that way.' The persons know they shouldn't feel depressed and rejected, but that doesn't make them feel better. It only increases the guilt and leaves them feeling worse.

"Another road block is the statement that 'All

things work together for good.' That is a wonderful Bible verse, but when it's dumped on a divorced person, it is like saying that there's something wrong with you. Apparently you don't realize that if only you have more faith you would feel better, but that ignores the reality of grief to be worked through over a period of time."

Parent-Child Pathos

"It is a bruising experience for newly divorced persons to deal with the children's grief, anger, hostility, and hurt," revealed one friend. "I have never heard of children who did not want their parents to get together again. And all too often the caring, conscientious child assumes that he or she carries responsibility for the divorce." Children from homes breaking apart or from broken homes need special and supportive friendship from church family members and neighbors.

The concept of divorce as a death that goes on dying also typifies the separation of parent and child. Michael Johnson captures this in "Moving On":

> The last piece of furniture was carried out
>   of the house this evening,
> Like a wounded soldier on a litter;
> And the house now is only a cluster of empty
>   cubicles.
> My footsteps call out from the four walls as
>   I turn one last time

To see:
him—cornsilk hair and laughter flowing free as he
  scampers from room to room,
I can hear the puppy barking at his heels . . .
My footsteps cry out again
As I turn and walk out the door.
Time can't be stopped—
  it keeps moving on
And the empty house
  has become my mind—
He's gone.

Individual Support

Phone calls from friends to divorced persons are reinforcing—especially from within the church family. Relationships with friends and relatives on the spouse's side dry up much faster than one anticipates. "We soon become the 'odd-person-out'—or we acquire the status of a fifth wheel," charged one friend. "Life has become a game of musical chairs. At social events everyone else gets a chair, but you seen to be left standing—alone."

Adaptability is crucial when you visit the newly divorced. For example, determine whether the other person wishes to say nothing of the divorce or needs to "talk a blue streak."

"Regardless of our new 'free' society," one friend explained, "most women divorcing over the age of 35 are not comfortable with initiating either conversation or invitations to single men. Yet, it is normal for males to invite women to dinner, to a show, or over to friends. So months can pass without any social interaction for women. After years of being a 'couple,' it is extremely difficult for a newly single woman to do anything alone. That is why maintaining casual, nonthreatening communication within the church, including some family invitations, is so helpful to the divorced person."

One person told of a friend's loving act. "Immediately after closing our home following my divorce, one friend surrounded me with acceptance. 'Come stay as long as you want. Feel free to do or not to do anything you want.' I slept most of three days, but she never intruded. Her help was unobtrusive and completely nondirective. She left every decision up to me. I appreciated it and started to grow in the process."

"I know you are hurting, and I really care about that—and if you want to talk about it, I'll listen." A divorced friend claimed this insightful approach was liberating because, in effect, someone told her, "Yes, your suffering is unique; it must be painful. I do care about you in the midst of it, and I'll gladly help if I can."

"That communicates a willingness to walk beside me, and listen, and console, and comfort me," she said. "In effect, my friend gets down in the pit with me. That's different than standing outside a pit and calling down to somebody, 'Get out of the pit' or 'You shouldn't be in the pit' or 'Don't you feel better because everything is going to work together for good now that you're in the pit!' Those approaches are painful to the one who is already suffering.

"If I am in the pit, to console means that you get down in the pit with me and declare, 'I care about you,' or it may be more appropriate for you just to listen to me—to hear how it feels to be in the pit, how dreadful it is. Before I can heal, I must have an opportunity to express my feelings to someone."

The healing process often is slow after a shattered marriage. Professional counseling may be needed. One recently divorced person expressed this thought: "Time is a healer, but there is so much hurt, bitterness, and anger with which to deal. This bitterness can damage the newly divorced as well as that person's relationships with friends or members of the opposite sex." Sometimes a few in-depth sessions with the pastor or a professional counselor can set the newly divorced person on the road toward recovery, but don't wait until a person is an emotional mess before suggesting some professional guidance.

"Tell your readers," emphasized another friend, "that they should initiate the contacts to help and comfort the divorced person, and they need to have patience with the recovery rate. One can't expect most separated persons to heal quickly. Only Christ and time working through the problem can heal the suffering. Be sure to let your divorced friend know you are thinking of and praying for him or her—it really helps."

Small Group Support

There is a real need for a supportive community spirit in the body of Christ—and that happens mainly within small groups. A large, diffuse group has more difficulty being "family." Events are needed that draw persons to intimate groups where they may share their concerns and be assured of acceptance. Small group work should become our basic relationship style in supporting the newly divorced.

A friend endorsed this thinking: "How much we need to be touched by others and how much we (especially men) try to ignore it! After being divorced and alone, I used to watch married couples touch each other's arms or squeeze each other's hand at the dinner table. I watched these natural, automatic gestures like a half-starved orphan peering through a candy-store window. You can't believe how wonderful an arm around the shoulder, a squeeze of the hand, or a good hug can feel after you're alone. A group of fellow believers is best equipped to offer this supportive, silent communion of love and concern."

Another individual said, "The one who brought me the most healing is a young friend in our church circle. After I'd misunderstood a comment of his and gotten uptight, he said, 'You need to hear something. You're still fearful of anything that even resembles rejection, but you need to know that I'm committed to our friendship.' Those were the most beautiful words I've ever heard in my life. They brought more wholeness than almost anything, and church members can say that too. We can say, 'We may fail you, but by the grace of God we're committed to you. We really want to be your friend and to support you.'" Another church member spoke of the reality of incarnational theology. "I know of the love of God because I see it in my friends. I can't feel God's hug, but I can feel theirs. A person who's gone through divorce needs that healing touch of church members as never before."

4
When There Is Imprisonment

I won't forget the first prisoner I met inside the county jail. She was a young woman, small, alert, perceptive. During my discussion with a group of inmates, her comments were among the most sensitive and thoughtful. "In here, real life stops the moment you enter the institution," she said. "All decisions are made for you. The only real life in the world is 'out there.' Outsiders are free to decide what to do and when. They choose whether or not to visit us. We're helpless about initiating such contacts. We just wait, hope, wait, and then worry what's wrong when someone doesn't come to visit."

Most prisoners I talked with agreed that life in a correctional institution is "unreal." The county jail's specialty seems to be suspense-filled waiting. Inmates are submerged in uncertainty about their future. When will my case be tried? Will I be released? Will I be sentenced to a short term here? Will I be sent to the state penitentiary? If so, for how long? The county jail is an alien and tense world, particularly for first-time offenders.

In contrast, state penitentiary inmates face certainties of tedium, apathy, and boredom. These are the consequences of an extended prison sentence—a dulling daily routine, isolation from family and friends, the loss of personal identity, and few meaningful decision-making opportunities.

Most of us are provoked and angered if others point out our errors or misdeeds. Those in prison have similar feelings, but their mistakes are publicized. In addition, they have lost their freedom. They react with bitterness toward imprisonment and maintain, "everything in here is negative."

External Support

Faithful support from visitors is important to prisoners. As one said, "Without support, we become lonely—and let me tell you, this is no place to be lonely!"

Promising a visit but failing to arrive confirms a negative bias that one can't trust others. As an inmate reported, "I'll tell you one thing that gets me. Some special friend is going to come and see you, and you think about it all day and all night and what you're going to say—and then, 'no show.' Boy, that's a cold, cold feeling!"

Be specific about when the inmate may expect you

to return. Don't promise another visit unless you will follow through.

Prepare to Share the "Real World"

If the prisoner wants to talk about himself or herself, don't interrupt. Listening is a helpful ministry. But many prisoners are weary of questions like, "What did you have for lunch?" or "How's everything going in here?" As one said, "I'm just existing in here; that's about it. The daily routine is monotonous. I think visitors assume we have a lot to do in here—but we don't. It's all dead in here." And then she continued, "Somehow in their visit, I want them to take me out of here. They can tell me about things that make me feel better, and I want them to be positive. For example, 'Hey, it snowed outside' (especially if you don't have an outside window), or 'Do you know what happened in school today?'—things that if you were home you'd know were happening. You want to hear all the things that go on out there."

Another inmate summarized similar feelings. "Outsiders need to know how to make a visit richly rewarding to us." This requires both agenda planning and flexibility. The inmate may or may not want to talk about himself or herself. Realize that everybody needs personal contact—a touch of the hands or a hug. Physical contact speaks acceptance and releases tension for one steeped in rejection.

A county prisoner suggested another form of

acceptance. He suggested that a visitor say on departing, "If you're on the street side, I'll look up and wave to you as I am leaving." The inmate continued, "I've seen guys who couldn't wait to get back to their area to wave—it's like it was just you and that person together. I had it happen to me once and thought it was the greatest day I've had in here."

Unhelpful Visiting

It's a bad visit when both parties tell about their troubles," stated one prisoner. "She may have troubles outside, but she doesn't need to bring them to me, because I've already got enough in here. That's just making both parties miserable."

Unwanted questions include asking when they are getting out. Neither do they like to be questioned about their crime, about previous convictions, or other incriminating topics. As one prisoner said, "If a person can't forget our past, it means they have not forgiven us." Another one stated, "Questioning us about the past only causes tensions."

Comments referred to as "downers" include: "Hey, girl, haven't you learned anything yet? How old are you now anyway? This is your umpteenth time in trouble. Why should we bother anymore—you're not learning anything."

Observations about prison clothing to women inmates can hurt. These include, "Wow, you don't fit your clothes very well, do you? Can't they give you something smaller—something with a belt? Don't they ever give you anything to wear besides that ugly uniform?"

Rejection from those who should be supportive "is one of the hardest things for a person in jail to take," claims one inmate. Another said, "If the visit is a negative, antagonistic, or tense experience, I take all this back with me. It bothers me. I get all uptight and strung out." Bitterness is typical of prison life and is easily fanned into strife. "After poor visits, I've seen many fellows come out of the visiting area, get in a fight, and wind up in the segregation area."

Another prisoner reported that visits from her family impress her as tokens. "They want to know if I'm learning anything, but they only come because they think they're supposed to—not because they care about me. My mother is so afraid that some of her friends will read my name in the paper and find out that we're related. I guess it's hard on her—but I know her attitude is hard on me."

Helpful Visits

"Being treated with respect and with dignity—being convinced that someone really cares about me—regardless of the past," said one inmate, "that's a good visit!"

Another prisoner said, "You really want people to come in and be positive with you and strike up a conversation. It could be about the moon you saw, and you can visualize it for me. Or you can take me for a trip in the park and tell me how the kids swung for the first time. That's great—that's something everybody can look forward to—and you can go back in there and still feel good."

"The best thing for me is encouragement—knowing that somebody's backing me up. I also need the reassurance that I'm still a part of something positive, because everything in here is negative—we're not dealing with the real world here. A good visit leaves you relieved."

"What's most helpful in a visit is that they come—whether they say anything or not. Just being here is showing that they care, and there's something kind of spiritual about it if they'll grab hold of my hands—it tells me I'm really accepted as a person—I'm really not an untouchable. How they look at me can give me confidence—and you got to build up our confidence!"

"A good visit for me is their talking about the family life I'm missing, what they're doing day by day—shearing the sheep—planting the corn—painting the house—I enjoy hearing about them and the life because I can't share that. I want to know about what I can't see—what I can't feel."

"It's helpful if visitors let me know ahead of time that they're coming, so I can be ready for them—and anticipate the visit."

"If someone tells me the leaves are turning a really pretty color on the hillside, now that's a good visit for me. I like if people tell me, "Here's what is going on outside'—I can't see it for myself, and I miss so much—I don't know nothin' in the real world unless somebody tells me."

And another prisoner added, "There may be beauty out there, but we don't touch it; we don't smell it—it's there, but we never get to it. And you've got to be able to touch—you can say that you care about someone, but it's a lot more convincing and human if you can tell them by touching."

"It's strange, but the visits from those who are not family or close friends can be the most satisfying. First, they don't have to come, so they must want to. Then when they leave, it's not the emotional bummer you experience when your loved ones go back out to freedom and you go back down the corridor. It doesn't bother as much—you've had a good communication with someone who cares—this makes a good visit."

Communication by Letters

"My sister writes each month," complains one inmate, "and says, 'The reason I don't write more is that I don't have anything to say. So what's going on with you in there?' Well, she's out in the *real* world where things are happening. I told her to pick up a pencil and start writing anything that's on her mind—anything—anything. Here I wait till the mailman comes, but nothin'—*every* day, I know I ain't going to expect nothin'. Ain't a day going by but I sit up waiting for him to go by—and nothin'!"

"My old lady always writes the same thing—she

writes and says, 'When you gettin' out?' Well, they gave me seven years in the joint, and I've been here four and a half years and she says, 'When you gettin' out?'"

"I like the positive things people say. When they write and say the expenses are too high this month, what do they think I ought to do—there's nothing I can do in here—a guy can only do so much inside these walls."

"When I write to someone, I tell them that I have a hard time thinking of news—every day is the same. So I ask them to ask me questions, so I can write about something they don't know about, and it works great. I get the questioningest letters you ever saw—it makes me think they're interested."

"It's not helpful for a wife or girl friend to write about what they did over the week-end—or the nights they go out."

"My lady friend doesn't ever ask me about what I do in here anymore. I wrote and told her once, and then said, 'When you visit me or write to me don't ever ask me what I'm doing in here because I don't want to talk about it.' And I don't want to hear all her 'downs'—I've got enough of my own—and she understands that now. She gives me a lot of feedback on my last letter—she reads the emotions between the lines, and it helps a lot. So my spirit is really with her all the time. I think that in getting and writing letters you can express your feelings better than in a visit. You can really let your feelings out. I'm in the cell by myself and there's no one here to say, 'Hey, don't say that.' There's no interruptions, no interferences. You have plenty of time to react to their feelings—more than in a 20-minute visit."

"When I hear about serious problems at home, I get all uptight, because I'm helpless to do anything about it from in here. For a couple of days the news kept bothering me, but not really realizing it was, I ended up getting in a fight—and it changed my custody. So when they write about serious problems, it reacts really deep, because you can't do anything about it—there's not a thing you can do about it right now—except maybe a prayer—but a lot of people don't secure themselves in that."

"The worst letter you can get is a 'Dear John' letter. That's when your wife or your girl friend writes you off with 'OK, baby. You're in jail now, and you can go it on your own.' When I was turned off by my lady, I got so frustrated—I was like insane for a while in my thinking! When a man's already under stress and someone puts more burden on him, it makes him worse. That's just common sense."

A positive letter you write to a prisoner can be reread and savored time and time again. If you wish to befriend an inmate with correspondence, encourage him or her to write to you and then respond faithfully and promptly.

Accentuate the Positive

One prisoner smiled as he told me, "I think the biggest thrill that a guy or a woman gets in here is when someone comes up and gives a compliment. Even if it's only, 'Well, gee, you got a good-looking haircut.'"

A woman prisoner followed the compliment theme with, "That's very true. My husband came up to see me last night and the first thing he said was 'You look good'—not caring that I only weigh 80 pounds now and I'm almost dead. It's a fact that I did have a smile on my face because he was there. The minute you see a visitor, you automatically get a glow to you. And the first time he says, 'Hey, it's all right. No matter what the circumstances, I'm staying right beside you.' Well, I almost went out of my skin. I know what I did to put myself in here, but he never brought it up once. It was just the fact that he said things that would make me feel good. It made me say, 'If you ever go down, I'll be there.' And that's the kind of support people here want and look forward to. You need a certain type of bond when it's time to get out of here—somebody that'll really be waiting for you when you come out—and they better be there—or they shouldn't ever make the promise!"

Another inmate continued on the topic of "someone saying good things about you." He added, "When you have positive contact, you go back to your cell and you've got that good feeling inside you. No matter what anybody says to you, you've got that great sensation inside, and you've lost that tension. Stress just seems to melt away. But if you have a negative visit, it plays on your thoughts, and you're all uptight. Then somebody says something like, 'Hey, how did it go?' and you're liable to bust him one."

The implications to guide visitors seem clear. Encourage the prisoner to talk. Listen carefully. Answer all questions honestly, clearly, and concisely. Search for anything positive you can recognize and commend. Express sincere, authentic praise. When a prisoner exists in a negative environment, even a little compliment can last a long time—and will help to heal a badly bruised self-concept. Possibly Paul summarized the situation best when he said: "Finally, brethren, whatever is true, whatever is honorable, whatever is just, whatever is pure, whatever is lovely, whatever is gracious, if there is any excellence, if there is anything worthy of praise, think about these things" (Philippians 4:8 RSV).

Grace, Faith, and the Future

A first step in understanding God's acceptance is for a prisoner to see Christ's love personalized in a brother or sister who accepts the prisoner unconditionally. One inmate said, "You've got to be known and accepted as a person by someone. In here you're waiting, and you're waiting, and you're waiting, and usually you don't know if anybody cares."

Inquire about the inmate's future plans. What would he or she really want to do? Talk about alternative ways in which realistic goals might be achieved.

Visitors need wisdom and good judgment in relation to sharing their faith. Prisoners will best comprehend your faith from your actions, not your words. As a visitor be prepared to share your faith naturally—but try to discern and follow, not lead the Holy Spirit's promptings. Simply reveal that God's grace in Christ is more than adequate to obliterate every sin of any believer inside or outside prison. Pray earnestly for those you visit. Tell them of your prayers.

If an inmate would like Christian reading materials, inform the prison chaplain of the request. Suggest that he or she write to the International Prison Ministry, Box 63, Dallas, Tex. 75221. At a prisoner's request, the organization will send a free Bible. A Bible dictionary and a concordance by Cruden also can be requested and will be sent postpaid. "Life-Changing Books" are available in many chaplain's offices.

Avoid making promises to do more for an inmate that you can accomplish. Let the person realize that you, being human, could let him or her down. Instead, direct the prisoner's faith toward God.

As a brochure entitled "How Christians Can Be Involved in Jail and Prison Ministry" wisely states, "Don't be discouraged. Do your best. Pray.... Expect great things to be accomplished.... Leave the results to God."

5

The Challenge

Concern about saying the "wrong thing" hinders many of us from visiting friends afflicted with illness, death, divorce, or imprisonment. The following guidelines can inspire us to minister with increased confidence to individuals whose lives are disordered.

Oral Communication

Talking

Worrying about what to say often results from our feeling obligated to fill every quiet moment in a conversation with words. This attitude counteracts meaningful communication. Silence between friends can be a rewarding experience. It confirms the existence of deep understanding and the acceptance of other persons just as they are. Silence on our part allows the one visited an opportunity to express his or her feelings and concerns—an essential ingredient in the healing process.

At the same time, those visited like to hear of happy or humorous incidents in the lives of family and friends. This provides them time away from their present affliction. Refrain, however, from prying into your friend's "personal property"—details of the illness, reasons for being in jail, determinants of divorce, etc. And spare your friend unrequested, easy solutions for complex, personal problems.

Listening

A friend told me, "Before I can heal, I must have an opportunity to express my feelings to someone." Patient listening is our most effective tool for ministering to an acquaintance in distress. It allows an individual to sort through feelings, confusions, and internal conflicts that need resolution in the healing process. As a visitor, we need to say little. It is helpful, though, to repeat or briefly summarize major points in our own words. This approach with no implied judgment confirms the fact that we understand and accept what the other person is saying.

Empty Words

Regardless of the sincerity with which one says, "If there's anything I can do, please let me know," overuse has tarnished the authenticity of this phrase. It's better to say nothing about helping than to use what now seems to be a cliche. Instead, suggest a specific service activity and offer that to your friend.

Taboo Words

Particular words, phrases, or names heighten our anxiety about saying the wrong thing. We tend to shun words such as cancer, dying, death, divorce, prison, and penitentiary. Such deliberate censorship is unhelpful when talking with individuals who need to face and not avoid the realities in their lives.

The temptation is strong to exclude the dead person's name when talking with a survivor. We fear we may provoke sadness by reminding the survivor of his or her loss. Actually, the one we seek to protect from pain regularly thinks of and cherishes memories about that person. Use your dead friend's name in natural conversation as you recall previous experiences together. This helps the survivor's adjustment to life alone.

Written Communication

Writing to one who is lonely has several advantages. Distance is not a barrier. We benefit by having more time to formulate our thoughts. And it is usually easier to express personal feelings, convictions, or a witness in a letter. More significant, the one who receives it may save the message for rereading whenever desired.

Behavioral Communication

Studies recognize the enormous impact of nonverbal communication. For example, if others sense a contradiction between what we say and what we do, their inclination is to believe our actions to be more reliable than verbal statements.

To a troubled person, our physical presence or absence speaks more eloquently than words. Our sharing of unhurried, personal time may be the choicest gift we can bestow on a lonely individual, and a nonverbal smile can be a warm, uplifting gift. The same is true with physical touch—a squeeze of the hand for a patient unable to speak, holding a friend's hand during prayer, and an arm around the shoulder or a hug for the bereaved, newly divorced, or imprisoned. Far more compelling than words, these physical contacts proclaim our unity with those overburdened with distress.

Sensitivity to Feelings

When visiting the afflicted, an alert awareness to every aspect of the immediate situation is essential. Each individual differs significantly from other persons. Applying a single set of guidelines to every situation is precarious at best. During different visits, the distressed person may even respond in dissimilar ways.

Compassion, not pity, is appropriate when calling on the ill, bereaved, divorced, or imprisoned. "Feeling with" another person involves empathy, a mutual sharing of suffering or joy—crying or laughing. Such compassion affirms nonverbally, "Your feelings are

OK. It is permissible to express them to me. I understand and accept you completely, just as you are."

Feelings of guilt and shame are often associated with divorce and imprisonment. They may even be linked with cases of illness and death. The guilt reaction typically results in rejection of self, rejection of others, and rejection of God. The Christian message of absolute forgiveness and total acceptance by God is the antidote for self-depreciating guilt. To withhold this word of forgiveness is to deny release and joy to those we aim to help.

Loneliness is a common heartache that afflicts the ill, the bereaved, the divorced, and the imprisoned. An onslaught of visits, letters, and invitations arrives just after the crisis. The drought that follows can be alleviated by considerate persons who continue to befriend the lonely when relatives have returned to their homes and associates have resumed their previous daily activities.

Support and Encouragement

In organizations, everybody's responsibility tends to become nobody's responsibility. Some individuals in the church family must be accountable for organizing support groups to enfold and minister to those engulfed by loneliness. Members who have experienced and overcome such isolation may be premium candidates to undergird and nurture the hurting.

Most state and federal prisons provide chaplaincy

programs and religious services for their 309,000 inmates. More than three times as many persons (over 1,000,000) spend some time each year in city or county jails. Most of these jails have no chaplain or regular religious services. This predicament highlights one of the greatest visitation needs in our nation. The phrase, "Out of sight, out of mind" appears to characterize our reaction to this challenge.

Children, too, are neglected casualties of severely stressed parents. While adults suffer through illness, death, divorce, or imprisonment, their children's emotions churn and ferment. Youth also agonize with feelings of guilt, shame, anger, and hostility. Their emotions run deep, and some withdraw in isolation. Others demand attention, reassurance, and love for their fragmented lives. This complex demand may be partially met if children experience the security of some consistent, supportive love from members in their church family.

William James said that the greatest need people have is to be appreciated. This is vividly obvious as we work with egos damaged by feelings of guilt, shame, and inadequacy. Search out and comment on anything positive you can discover about the person visited. This is an important ministry that counteracts chronic feelings of inadequacy and rejection. Paul's suggestion that we fill our minds with things that are good and that deserve praise (cf. Philippians 4:8) outlines the recommended approach to those who suffer discouragements.

Summary

Probably not one of us ever will qualify in all respects as the ideal visitor. Apprehension about personal visiting skills makes Cardinal Newman's observation pertinent where he says that nothing would ever get done if we waited till it was done so well that no one could fault it in any way. This concept is reinforced in another saying, "How silent the woods would be if only the best birds sang." And how void of friendships the lonely would be if only experts responded to their visitation needs!

The man or woman of God daring to reach out in a visiting venture will never confront that challenge alone. God's presence will be tangible in the midst of each ministering effort, especially if our attitude is similar to that of John, who said, "He must increase but I must decrease" (John 3:30 KJV). Those who need your presence will sense beyond any doubt that you really care, love, and accept them just as they are. And they will better comprehend God's love, because they see it personalized not only in what you say but also in what you do.

Permissions

The Bible text in this publication marked TEV is from the Good News Bible, the Bible in TODAY'S ENGLISH VERSION. Copyright © American Bible Society 1966, 1971, 1976. Used by permission.

Scripture quotations marked RSV are from the Revised Standard Version of the Bible, copyrighted 1946, 1952, © 1971, 1973 by the Division of Christian Education of the National Council of the Churches of Christ in the U.S.A., and used by permission.

Paul Tournier. *The Meaning of Gifts* (Richmond, VA: John Knox Press, 1965)

The poem on p. 23 is from Dorothy Hsu's book, *Mending* (Elgin, IL: David C. Cook Publishing Company, 1979). Used by permission.

The poems on pp. 30, 31, and 33 are by Michael Johnson. From *Winter: A Collection of Poems on Divorce and Loneliness* (unpublished). Used by permission.